THE LIGHT OF WHAT COMES AFTER

The Light of
What Comes After

JEN TOWN

BAUHAN PUBLISHING
PETERBOROUGH NEW HAMPSHIRE
2018

ISBN: 978 087233 256 0

Library of Congress Cataloging in Publication Control Number: 2018008461

For information on the May Sarton New Hampshire Poetry Prize:
http://www.bauhanpublishing.com/may-sarton-prize/

To contact Jen Town:
http://jentown.com

Book design by Kirsty Anderson
Cover design by Henry James
Cover photo by Jason Gray

PO BOX 117 PETERBOROUGH NEW HAMPSHIRE 03458

603-567-4430

WWW.BAUHANPUBLISHING.COM

Follow us on Facebook and Twitter – @bauhanpub

MANUFACTURED IN THE UNITED STATES OF AMERICA

To my parents
Michael and Carolyn Town
for their love and support

CONTENTS

ONE: SHORT AUTOBIOGRAPHY ON TIPTOES

The Lily Dale Psychics Promised You	11
Invisible Self-Portraits in a Dark Room	12
Telling the Future on Paradise Island	14
Modes of Travel	15
My Heart after the Cyclone	16
In the Poem about Birds	17
In the Silent City She's Yearned For	19
How Well We Do Stars	20
Epithalamium in the City of Saints and Sinners	22
Short Autobiography on Tiptoes	23

TWO: THE WHIMSICAL CHARM OF MY MELANCHOLY

The Whimsical Charm of My Melancholy	27
Love Poem in the Vocabulary of Fruit	28
The Couple in the Picture Show	29
Your Pearls before Swine	31
Time Passed as Is Its Wont	32
A Syllabary of Birds	33
How Will I Ever Leave	34
My Love in the Manner of Soviet Espionage	35
Swain	37
A Tale of Cause and Effect	38
In the Province of Sleep: A Vignette	39
Needles Piercing Cloth	40

THREE: LIFE IN THE NEXT CENTURY

Life in the Next Century   45

Happy Happenstance   46

O Little Milk Toast   48

Hail to the Bloomers   50

Dear Customer   51

Spun   53

The Kitchen Drawers Spilleth Over   54

Charming   55

Faunapocalypse   56

The Age of Science   58

The Stars' Light Finding Us from the Deep Past   59

Who's Accountable in the Age of the Soapbox   60

The Colors of Youth and Wealth   62

In a Field of Snow between Two Horses   63

Some Brief Form of Happiness   65

Ode to the Ominous House of Salt   66

The Museum of Failure Has Many Rooms   68

Acknowledgments   70

SHORT AUTOBIOGRAPHY ON TIPTOES

As in childhood we live sweeping close to the sky, and now, what dawn is this.
—Anne Carson

The Lily Dale Psychics Promised You

Each day will be the soft
susurrations of silk
against a window ledge.

All your cakes will rise bloom-like
over their cake pans and you'll own
all the proper lawn-care products. But

one day traveling through the landscape
of your birth, you'll cup air
in your palm out the car window,

waving to where you left your childhood,
and under the colored glass
that has become your life, you'll feel

unease—like smoke
from an unseen cigar. But that's
all. You'll keep driving. The days

will swallow you, and the many days
afterward, like coins dropped
into a fountain, with the ease of wishing.

Invisible Self-Portraits in a Dark Room

after Ellen Harvey's Invisible Self-Portraits (framed), 2007

Hear me. I am
a fraud. Little me
in a rocking chair
under my self-
portraits in gilded
frames. Here I am—
a frantic blur, a flash
of light that leaves
your retinas stunned.
I float in your vision
everywhere you turn.

I believe myself to be
a sympathetic character
but formed to what
purpose, I'm not sure.

And you are the type,
I know, who asks
too many questions.

In this one, I hold
a plate of cherries
on the verge of rot.

Classic still life—that's
what the critics will say.
In all of these
invisibility symbolizes
an exploration
of death and its many
well-loved themes.
In all of these I am
frantic with some great loss.

In this one, above me
hangs a chandelier
strung with pearls,
and in this one,
I'm behind the fire.
Here, I shoot
like a rocket
out of the frame.

Telling the Future on Paradise Island

You'll always be one spoon
short of a set. You'll masquerade

as a dentist at parties and find it
difficult to believe there's a heaven.

The car alarm will go off *again*.

You'll race to the window
in your negligee, cursing. You'll find

it easy to adapt to the cold. To
the heat. You'll moonlight

as an astronaut—why not?
You'll contemplate the dead oregano

in your garden, blame the dog
for digging things up. You'll

fall in love with the man
in this poem, the soft hairs

on his chest. He'll die
at sea and in the bright noon

of the hereafter, he'll look for you—
or he won't—in all the wrong places.

Modes of Travel

From Paris to Madrid is a winding coil of train tracks and engines, the much-machineried world etched into hillside and valley. Subway clatter and airplane contrails. You can get from here to there in a few hours. And you do—and when you step off the train, holding your hat onto your head, you've become an anachronism. You're looking for the old world, to be swept up in it all, the turning of the centuries. You fan yourself with your hand, pick up your suitcase, and step off the station onto cobblestone. Who do you think you've come here to be? The echo of your shoes on the road is the racket of gunshots fired off in celebration of your arrival.

My Heart after the Cyclone

I walk to the window,
wait beside the velvet
curtains—lashes aflutter.

The door clicks
open to reveal
the Technicolor marvelous,

the glittering do-gooder
and his crystal ball, the hapless
king of I-meant-well. *I see,*

he says, *you're faint
of heart.* Tell me something
I don't know: why the streets

sometimes quiver
like a lower lip
when I'm out walking;

why I won't shake hands
with those I meet; why
the streetlight's corona fills

with moths. In the distance, sirens—
the Emerald City on its knees,
burning. How beautiful it is from here.

In the Poem about Birds

There were many birds
on clotheslines   left out to dry

There was the ominous feeling of more
rain to come   In the poem

about birds   you are one stippled
feather away from a flock

you defrocked & left
your sweet & multicolored

robes lying about the fountain
Somewhere a woman plays

the harpsichord   wearing
the face of an angel   Call her

egret   her skin
the color of bleached bone

If this is fairy tale   where
are the stones leading us home

We wear regret   always
a second flesh   If this is

myth   sing me
again songbird   the one

about the rising oceans
the olive branch you plucked

from waves & carried
away in your weary mouth

In the Silent City She's Yearned For

She'll find herself here, in the silent city
she's yearned for, touching its sooty surfaces

while its students of argyle and innocence
traipse along, toting their heavy bags. Under the pavement, pavement,

and under the dirt, bones, the silt of ancient rivers.
She's standing on the centuries. She's standing in someone's

small village. She'll never be alone here. The children
                              walk by with their Italian ices,
the wind smells of exhaust, of baking bread. With night coming on,

where will she go? The park is full of the homeless,
                      the shops on High have closed. Her apartment,
its light burning, seems to belong to someone else.

She'll look into her own window, press her nose
                  to the warmth. A stranger walks by,
talking into his hand, promises *I'll look for you.*
                  But, mister, how will you know who you've found?

How Well We Do Stars

The night is our pale pink
oyster, our candelabra,
a dimly lit theatre
of dreams. *You heard me.*

We'll find something witty to say,
easy repartee, *Why hello there.* Later we'll
take off all our
predilections, *tabula romantic,*

we'll start the evening over
and over and over again,
leave desire and decorum
to their tug and pull, step across

the death mask of melancholy
lit like a jack-o'-lantern
on the city street. Let me
point out something you've not seen.

Stand here. No, closer.
See all the satellites blinking
(how well we do stars now—
mimic their effulgent gaze,

their ancient eyes). I'll take
your hands, place them *here*
and *here*. That's it. Where I come
from we call this fore-

shadowing, the rest
of the evening
lit up in our brains
like a movie marquee.

Epithalamium in the City of Saints and Sinners

Her ichor spilled all over the freesia. What a mess.
All better after a little tart's bath in the park fountain.
Say, this is a bad scene. Let's get outta here.

My darling, he mumbled,
you have the loveliest clavicle I've ever seen. I could
swim out to the white shores of your breasts.

Please, she said, *I beg of you, stop.*   *I wore my new dress for this,*

her loneliness freshly laundered. But isn't loneliness
loss in a different suit? She holds out
her cigarette like a wineglass. *Inside*

I'm a small child sliding out of my chair,
under the kitchen table. His body, that hirsute
reliquary: he boasts he once slept with
the fishes. *It seemed like a good idea at the time.*
Doesn't everything? Mr. Tall-Dark-and-Handsome

slips something sparkly onto her finger, and they're
pronounced. What follows is the ceremonial
casting away of her former self, the cutting of coattails
and tossing of fruits, while small girls in pastels
do somersaults down the aisle.

Short Autobiography on Tiptoes

She put down her rending
        of garments and teeth-gnashing to believe

in the essential good. She was taught to yield
        to the heart's wayward desires.

She was raised in the Rah Rah School
        of frosting and first snows. When young,

        she'd been accused of being too much and always
in earnest. In the Broadway version of her life, someone asks

May I kiss you now? Then the lights
        fade to black. There will always be some boy
waiting for her in the darkened wings

of her mind. When relaying poignant details over dinner,
she leaves the truth out. When older,
        she'll realize all these years she's been held together

        by mascara and string. She's always in a hurry.
There was a time in her life when she would agree to anything.

THE WHIMSICAL CHARM OF MY MELANCHOLY

. . . the lovers
blizzarded in their separate bodies like settlers in cabins—
—Priscilla Sneff

The Whimsical Charm of My Melancholy

I've always been the one
          standing in the rain, breathless, staring
through the lit windows of your boudoir. Call it
          love à la mode, love of grand gestures,

love à la the cinema. I'll bring you a basket
          of ripe persimmons, offer you slivers
the size of my pinky, because *nothing
          says lovin'* like overripe fruit. It'd be best,

though, if you'd turn away, nothing more
          poignant than love unrequited, love
                    lost, love's labors
all for naught. In the street, couples dance
          the tarantella, and the night smells like the chic

          blooms of the dogwood trees that line
the street where you live, where I wait
                    in solemn prayer
          like some saint, say, St. Philip

          of the many splendid things
and the brokenhearted. It's a wonder. We meet,
          become one. At least

that's the story. O there are the flutes,
                    right on cue. It's all
too much really. I must leave before I break
          into song.

Love Poem in the Vocabulary of Fruit

She said   my honey
             berry   my tomatillo
you come to the marrow

of my mock orange   Who gives
     a blue fig what sweetsop we sing to
each other on this living rock   We love

    down to the rhubarb
                  the sweet cup
    of the cushaw   Let your papaw
and mamme think what they want

    Let the granny smiths
of the world *tsk-tsk* themselves
        into eternity   We'll make

like the bitter marasca   a sweet liquor
    the single seed in the scarlet palm

                what a windfall
we'll yield
Harvested, we'll harvest

The Couple in the Picture Show

And what now? she wanted to know,
licking a stamp onto an envelope.

The children's ice skates
hung in the shed with ropes of garlic
and a large smoked ham. Dried bunches of coriander

and a blue pot. *My domesticity*. She had tried
her hand at the cookery; she had sewn
cotton undies till her hands ached. Here she was,

up nights with a colicky baby, the cat's
big eyes staring at her from a dark corner.

It was a time for sacrifice. She had become practiced
at taking things away from herself—small things

she loved: her favorite thimble, the bluebells
her little son had picked. She eschewed

the éclairs of her youth, walked past
the bakery with its neatly organized displays.

She gazed longingly at Lady Liberty
and her crown of stars.

This was the silver screen era, her heart a big band
with all its dazzle, a lounge singer in sequins.

She knew that planes came and went
every few seconds at airports around the world.

There was a heavy ocean of human
guilt through which the world
drifted. Enter

her hunkered-down darling, arms full of newspapers
with banner headlines—stories
in a tailspin toward her.

Your Pearls before Swine

" . . . *neither cast ye your pearls before swine,*
lest they trample them under their feet,
and turn again and rend you."

—Matthew 7:6

You're broken,
                    windmilled,
your little boysenberries'
bedrock. I'm the flocked

tilefish in the bathysphere,
the taunt in the hollow of the pen,
            five butterfly orchards
spreading blue wingdings

to rise out of your scarcities, dark handsome
            pilferer rifling
through your pale lady underthings,
dirty fingerlings fondling
a strandline of pearly everlastings;

your throat, sweet bread, and I
a stone bramble tricked up
            like a cherry tree. I'm the bodkin
you feel while wearing your fox
petticoats. My hearse is in my hand:
in touch, I love: in loving, own.

Time Passed as Is Its Wont

You love a man from years ago, love his laugh rising through murky
waters, coming toward you from a great distance. He held it against
you—how the wind blew slantways in this frigid place to which you
brought him, all the people walking bent over. Now you understand
the world as a litany of *not here, not here*. The song of his absence hums
at you, like a cricket in a cage in the city inside you, which he haunts,
and which you'll wake to, the streets a stain the heart's rendered from air.

A Syllabary of Birds

How far is *sparrow* from *sorrow*—
the house sorrow that swoops in
and makes for itself a nest of troubles—

and between *cardinal* and *nail*—
only *i*—upon which everything
hangs. Read in *red*

the color of rust, of love
and disease. And where
swallow leaves off begins

a swell of words, unloosed.
In the lark's frail wings
we see joy, no small thing,

and above us the birds
mark their own kingdom
while we make of them

our own lexicon—the mourning dove's
somber call a *voice*, we say,
rising in song, having no other word for it.

How Will I Ever Leave

By way of an ending, she offered
the porch swing they'd painted yellow,

and the memory of the upstairs murmur,
the furnace running full-blast. And now

Who are you? she wondered. Staring up
the height of him,

she remembered being small,
talking softly to herself in the garden

while adults drank sun tea
on the stoop. But that's all over now—

that house entropic even in her imaginings—
door frames toppled like Lincoln logs.

There's nothing to walk through, she thought.
How will I ever leave?

My Love in the Manner of Soviet Espionage

The day made movements to the west,
like a ship, lacquered and flag-waved.

I wanted a hearty borscht and a babushka,
and one of those matryoshka dolls.
I slipped my bare feet into violet shoes
and the mirror said I was ready.

And there was Helga, Hilda, and whoever,
kneading with their forearms into
bread that grew like love

and rose like a bubble
to the surface of the late afternoon,
which gleamed like a serving dish
in the poem which is neatly folded
and scented, laundered with lavender.

But there were colder times to come,
of course. On the tundra, the wind
was having a field day. Someone called out
in a language hearty as stew. All I wanted
was to sit in some dark corner
and whisper to you my Russian love phrases.

But first I had to walk stone streets
until my feet swelled; I had to find
inhospitable dark alleys. I had to swig
something fiery and tear bread into tiny pieces
while I waited for you with a slip
of a message you'd burn after I'd gone.

Swain

On the lea the wind winnows down

a bed of rock. Here our earthly

embellishments: a cairn, a salt cellar, the fleshy

leaves of spring. Everything: the cowslip

and cornfoot coroneted.

A dash of coriander to sweeten the pot.

Must we leave all this behind?

From the grasses we see stratus

and cumulonimbus. Tomorrow,

we'll go to the city. He'll try his hand

at haberdashery; I'll soak his white linens

in water and ash. We'll sleep in

our sundry past.

A Tale of Cause and Effect

I've been one laugh short of a miracle. My stockings have runs. I've been most often wrong about others. I've looked a man in the eyes searching for his childhood: I saw apples in a wheelbarrow set out to rot. When we moved to the city, he stopped touching me. Now there's gray—it grows on buildings—it seeps into the water system—we drink it day after day. It sluices into our cells.

In the Province of Sleep: A Vignette

The women twist in their designer stilettos. There are too many of us, someone mutters. Everyone carries their beloved tucked under one arm like a newspaper. *And earlier:* Please flip that—it's burning. Iron that. Untangle yourself, please. *Later on:* The man with the mile-high eyebrows prepares remarks. His wife is tall and angular like a thistle. What do you want? With cream? she asks. Let's hide here until it's over, I tell you. Until the story has unwound itself. Until everyone's left to their yawning.

Needles Piercing Cloth

It was a world of décolletage,
the diaphanous thrills

of forgetting—lily skin
draped in spring and sugar

sifting through fingers—pollen's
golden settling on footstool

and ottoman, pie rack
and icebox. A world of garden

walls aflame with bloom. Birds
outdid each other in trilling;

Bartlett pears grew rounder
on the windowsill,

and yet: inside we drifted like
smoked bees in a silence

through which clocks
ticked, sound of silver needles

piercing cloth. On our table
last year's harvest reappeared

as wine. The air outside
a vignette, and inside,

lives in dénouement:
near the end of our story, and falling.

LIFE IN THE NEXT CENTURY

All the untidy activity continues,
awful but cheerful.
—Elizabeth Bishop

Life in the Next Century

The prophet said *My belly is full*
of the next century's honeybees:

hear them
and be comforted. We had reckoned

with malaria. We dressed the women
in their finest cowgirl boots,

asked the men to tighten their ties
to nooses. We maintained

the sordid spectacle. Many of us became
the unwilling third party, the unwitting

accomplice left holding the bag. We were
looking for the next

dime-store visionary. When we tucked
our children in, we set their mobiles

to the mechanics of murder, to spin
like propellers. Our innocents, they
shrieked with delight and despair.

Happy Happenstance

It's one of those days, where May
snows petals, and happiness

looms overhead like a storm
cloud, the train whistle

a distant flute carved into air. All
the morning glories grow

at an alarming rate. The dust you kick up
comes back to you as cardamom.

You want to keep this: five-fingered
happiness, exquisite thievery, this

moment you've hijacked, hitchhiked
out of some gloomy story about, oh,

the death of the village's only goat, or
the efficient breaking of your too-red

heart. You think you'll pay for your
petty crimes, for the thoughtless

humming while shredding
the frothy dandelions, for the shoulders

you leaned against ever so
briefly. You'll remember

the song playing when everything
changed with a *whoosh*.

O Little Milk Toast

Little milk toast,
you gum the world
apart—tell me why
I'm in such throes of terror,
pouting in the asters,
putting up the boarders
in their third-rate rooms,
whispering *Nighty night*.
There's this story
and that, and in between
a world of sleep
and moonlighting,
the city's sleepwalking
inhabitants in sequins.
I'm a whirligig fueled
by legal stimulants
and fine dining, rotating
like a ballerina
in a music box. All
my fusty finery,
unfashionable hats
and silken scarves
can't trick me up
into the whimsical adult
I've longed to be.

I've been lied to
by the authorities,
and inside I'm light-years
younger than I appear.
Here I am,
which is where? I need
to know.

Hail to the Bloomers

She remembers requiring something pretty for her hair, and thinking *In the future won't we all be bald?* So much of anatomy and appearance is built on impracticalities. Progress has been a process of deletion. As in— gone went the hoopskirts, gone went the corsets, freedom a shapeless thing. Then there were the walking-the-streets rallies, the golden-hued ribbons and sashes—she was the belle of the suffragist ball. When she curtsied, everyone sang "Hail to the Bloomers." Things were gathering speed now: introducing the electric iron, the electric washer and dryer—clotheslines arcane as the butter churn. What would the air do now? It still blew hot and strong as before. Better to move the garbage down the street with—the suddenly abandoned street.

Dear Customer

We at the Office of the Ineffable
        call this moment *betrayal*. Imagine
your youngest daughter biting into a golden

delicious, only to find its ashes blowing
        from her frenzied mouth. Think *despise*—
the clenched fist at sunset, the already parched land,

another night without rain. Think *despair*—a basket
        of fruit turning to stone
in the sun. You've been abandoned

in the desert too often, and the rain dance
        of your prayers fills
the air with anything but rain.

It's then we crowd around you,
        promise you nothing
you can't get elsewhere, and for less,

the sky filling with dark clouds
        trembling like the startled wings
of ravens. When we opened the doors

we knew you'd line up for it,
        what you couldn't live without, the temptation
too much. Calm yourself with the word

circumstance. Pretend it's a happy accident
        and feign ignorance. Your debts
are more than you'll ever pay back.

Spun

I've often been accused of being a latchkey with no latch. I've written letters to the dead in the form of prayers and offered up oranges to the heavens. I've been incorrigible and slow-witted, caught up to and put upon. I have only one good side. In a morning that smells like carp and bagels, I feel the swarm of flies grow inconsolable behind me. The sun sharpens its knives, clears its throat. Before I know it, it's 3 a.m., then dawn. The poem closes like a jewelry box, a space in the air where the ballerina momentarily spun.

The Kitchen Drawers Spilleth Over

The lemon zester a scepter,
a sword, all those royal utensils

caught in silver sleep. The baby
pulls herself up, reaches toward

the glinting. Little spoon,
little mortar and pestle, I croon,

my kitchen drawers spilleth over,
forks lined up like pretty ladies. Dearest

egg cup, allow me to coddle you:
mothering hangs from my neck like

a dainty chain. The wayward knives
lay in a pile, sharks in a too small sea,

chockablock full of teeth. The baby plays
amidst all those sharp objects, round

eyes rosy mouth mouthing *uh-ohs*—
Uh-ohs all over. *Uh-ohs*, indeed.

Charming

Her father says *You're living in a fairy tale*. She is a pale daughter in white, her hair a powdered wig the color of mustard. She spins and her skirt catches the breeze, flounces around her. She likes the word *flounces*. She likes to spin. All around her the factory air, the charcoal smell of her father's unwashed clothes, the rivers churning through a city of silt. She's looking for a field to fall asleep in for one hundred years. She's looking to wake to someone's blowsy mouth. She gathers flowers by the roadside, weaves them into a rope for her escape. They shrivel and curl up into tiny fists, a string of fists that blow apart in the wind.

Faunapocalypse

In the furnace sits the trumpeter,
his face a mask of flames.

The sabled queen in her maleficence
is seized by the desire to sneeze

and outside the flora pulse thickly:
they are left to choke one another.

The vines develop teeth,
they develop hair, better for yanking.

Their low whistles at night would chill
the bones, if there were living bones left to hear.

The queen lives in a flower's imaginings.
A pilferer, she picks the petals

off the posies and eats them. *Pick a pocketful,*
she whispers and is off. She will eat up

all the to-do lists, complaining
the ink tastes of sulfur. The skeletons hunched

over their desks scratch out the day's ledgers,
columns adding up in the dark

in which ferns purr deeply.
Remember when this was called *myth*?

—the stars once handfuls
of salt tossed into the sky.

The Age of Science

Because the X-axis
is a continuous concrete surface,
but Y is an ongoing mystery—
because your fingers
are blades
of grass, and you
are broken, a man
with the periodic table
of elements scored into his back
offers to take you
to a great cathedral of learning
stacked with instruments
and monographs, its many rooms
of quiet hush and green
filtered light. Someone,
you say, should protect me
from the monstrous world,
but where in these books
is that written? A lit glass case
and inside an ancient nautilus
too heavy to lift to your ear.
What are you hoping to hear?
There is no sound in a shell:
what's there is *us*—
heartbeat, exhalation.

The Stars' Light Finding Us from the Deep Past

I dreamed a flood,
my house in the valley filling up
with the gushing forth, my small frame
seen clinging to the rooftop from
your many miles away. I am now
a small boat bopping in a placid lake,
waiting. Underneath, the drowned
live on: they shop for groceries
underwater. They push
their strollers through teeming schools
of silver fish. They grow magnificent
gardens of algae and coral. Here
in my sinkable ship, my molly browned,
I'm afraid for you—so far from home,
everything blown apart and up,
all the polar bears starving,
all the frogs growing their third eyes,
their webbed feet split like toes,
all the trees in their stillness moaning,
the forests' silent curses. None of this
needs you, and yet I do:
I need you to walk on these
deserted roads. I need you, boiling
your water potable, carrying with you
the secrets of fire. Here we are, no compass,
the stars' light finding us from the deep past.

Who's Accountable in the Age of the Soapbox

We are the dead. Our only true life is in the future.
—George Orwell, *1984*

O innocent persons
in question
mark: we're easy

currency, entirely
spendable & circling, *sua*
sponte, these little numbers:

a broker who cooks
the books, his holy
highness of the whiskey

bottles, investor in
carbon footprints,
lackey of the cream

of commerce, wearing our
frocks of folly in
the ivied hallways,

in the hollow
of language, circus
of caesuras. We carry

portmanteaus, our habiliments
hastily folded—a hiss
of steam will whisk wrinkles

from our negligees. Everything
we know is
make-believe. Let's

call the bees'
dying in the dusk
another form of dancing.

The Colors of Youth and Wealth

Where were you while heads of state wrote themselves into every constitution? Selecting your Sunday scarves, pale turquoise held against your skin, colors of youth and wealth. They blind like snow on a sunny day. Your friends have betrayed you to yourself. The trucks on your road shake the fragile windowpanes, glass longing to loosen from its frame, your furniture carved as though from ancient India—everything in your household longs to be from somewhere else. Yet your hands remember shaping things from clay, pots brought home to mother who placed them on shelves in a room where visitors would sit. All you wanted was to be at home when the weather grew sullen, to take summer trips to the coast, to sign your postcards *with love*. You'd settle for this life of *not knowing*—a quiet place where one can harbor the simple beliefs of childhood: rope swing, the disturbed pool swallowing your body whole.

In a Field of Snow between Two Horses

Autumn is a mole hole
the garden's vanishing into

winter a cartoon fox snooping
round the chicken coop

When fox when
when will you leave us be

your sniffing round shakes sleep from the hens
everywhere the scent of rotten primrose

The human heart's a fist pumping pain
through delicate veins

& the moon's a piece of machinery the Soviets
invented & replaced in the '50s

The real moon's tiny now
& fits in the fur-lined pocket

of a comrade in Moscow
who can't help but use its light to read by

Even he looks at the sky & thinks
Moon then *no*

In a field of snow between two horses
there is a bramble the man

knows is a kingdom of snow & hunger
Little birds with human hearts gorge

on frozen berries, their beady eyes calculating more
for me for me for me

Some Brief Form of Happiness

In the dim light of nine o'clock, everything softens. Everything feels blurry and underwater. This is how I like happiness: sweetly misremembered, night stretching out before us like a field. Like a blank piece of paper. Like taut satin. And, yes, like a road we'll saunter down, shoes off, batting lazily at the insects so that from far away it'll look like we're waving goodbye.

Ode to the Ominous House of Salt

Here's to nothing
      worthwhile. To the bright-red
         toaster sitting

in its crown of crumbs
      in the vacant kitchen—thanks

for nothing. Here's
to one more thing
      to avoid—the hand

outstretched in the back
      alley, everything stippled
         with germs, her hair

in its tidy bun, how the shrill
wind chimes make her teeth hurt. She'll stop

mopping to dream. She'll gather
pain in her trapezium—
      a taut string of it. Outdoors, the air

will smell like wet carpet and—
      What's that? Lavender. *Oh you,*
she exclaims, *you, and your promises,*
      and your boutonniere of primrose.

Out on the street a man breaks
       bottles with his voice and in the house
a little girl's rocking horse
       brays away the hours.

The Museum of Failure Has Many Rooms

after Ellen Harvey's Museum of Failure, 2007

This place is a maze through which
one's wanderings are infinite and bleak,
and largely unmappable, unreadable as
a closed book. I am not by nature

confessional and yet: I am
exactly what you think of me. I did so
want you to like me. I'll tell you
the tale of my youth

to make you understand:
I rode a red bicycle
to school. I was taunted as the young
are wont to be. When I grew up

I carried all this with me in a basket
in my arms, kept out of the rain.
And yet: to say all this is to miss
the essential something. To say one thing

is to leave something else unsaid. There are only
so many words in a breath. There
were days that smelled of fervent lilac,
of rain lifting off the sidewalks, turning to steam.

I am a fairy tale going off like a grenade
in your hands. I am an autobiography
shredding to bits and blowing away.
I am attempting to rewind myself.

I am always alive in the story
until the moment of my untimely demise.

Acknowledgments

I am grateful to the following journals in which versions of some of these poems appeared: *Bellingham Review, Botticelli Magazine, Cider Press Review, Crab Orchard Review, Lake Effect, Moon City Review, Prick of the Spindle, Spoon River Poetry Review, Unsplendid,* and *Waccamaw,*

I am indebted to my fellow students and teachers both at Penn State University and The Ohio State University, but especially Jason Gray, Ida Stewart, Natalie Shapero, Jon Chopan, and Kathy Fagan.

Deep gratitude to the team at Bauhan Publishing and to Jennifer Militello for choosing my manuscript as the winner of the 2017 May Sarton New Hampshire Poetry Prize.

Thanks to Jason Gray for the use of his beautiful photo for the cover art.

Special thanks to George Looney, my mentor and friend, for his unflagging support and belief in my work over the years.

And to my family, immediate and extended, to my parents (again), and to my brother, Ken Town, all of whom raised and made me.

And to Carrie Curtner, without whom, what would be the point?

The May Sarton New Hampshire Poetry Prize

The May Sarton New Hampshire Poetry Prize is named for May Sarton, the renowned novelist, memoirist, poet, and feminist (1912–1995) who lived for many years in Nelson, New Hampshire, not far from Peterborough, home of William L. Bauhan Publishing. In 1967, she approached Bauhan and asked him to publish her book of poetry, *As Does New Hampshire*. She wrote the collection to celebrate the bicentennial of Nelson, and dedicated it to the residents of the town.

May Sarton was a prolific writer of poetry, novels, and perhaps what she is best known for—nonfiction on growing older (*Recovering: A Journal, Journal of Solitude*, among others). She considered herself a poet first, though, and in honor of that and to celebrate the centenary of her birth in 2012, Sarah Bauhan, who inherited her father's small publishing company, launched the prize. (www.bauhanpublishing.com/may-sarton-prize)

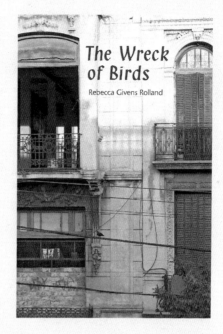

In *The Wreck of Birds*, the first winner of Bauhan Publishing's May Sarton New Hampshire Poetry Prize, Rebecca Givens Rolland embraces an assimilation of internal feeling and thought with circumstances of the natural world and the conflicts and triumphs of our human endeavors. Here, we discover a language that seeks to at once replicate and transcend experiences of loss and disaster, and together with the poet "we hope that such bold fates will not forget us." Even at the speaker's most vulnerable moments, when "Each word we'd spoken / scowls back, mirrored in barrels of wind" these personal poems insist on renewal. With daring honesty and formal skill, *The Wreck of Birds* achieves a revelatory otherness—what Keats called the "soul-making task" of poetry.

—Walter E. Butts, New Hampshire Poet Laureate (2009–2013), and author of *Cathedral of Nervous Horses: New and Selected Poems,* and *Sunday Evening at the Stardust Café*

Rebecca Givens Rolland is a speech-language pathologist and doctoral student at the Harvard Graduate School of Education. Her poetry has previously appeared in journals including *Colorado Review, American Letters & Commentary, Denver Quarterly, Witness, and the Cincinnati Review,* and she is the recipient of the Andrew W. Mellon Fellowship, the Clapp Fellowship from Yale University, an Academy of American Poets Prize, and the Dana Award.

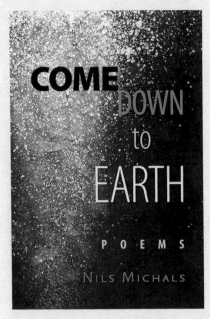

Nils Michals won the second May Sarton New Hampshire Poetry Prize in 2012, and has also written the book *Lure*, which won the Lena-Miles Wever Todd award in 2004. His poetry has been featured in *The Bacon Review, diode, White Whale Review, Bay Poetics, The Laurel Review* and *Sonora Review.* He lives in Santa Cruz, California and teaches at West Valley College.

Nils Michals is alternately healed and wounded by the tension between the timeless machinations of humankind and the modern machinery that lifts us beyond—and plunges us back to—our all-too-human, earthly selves. Supported by minimally narrative, page-oriented forms, his poems transcribe poetry's intangibles—love, loss, hope, a sense of the holy—in a language located somewhere between devotional and raw, but they mourn and celebrate as much of what is surreal in today's news as of what is familiar in the universal mysteries . . . *Come Down to Earth* is a 'long villa with every door thrown open' "

—Alice B. Fogel, New Hampshire Poet Laureate (2014-2019), and author of *Strange Terrain: A Poetry Handbook for The Reluctant Reader* and *Be That Empty*

David Koehn won the third May Sarton New Hampshire Poetry Prize in 2013. His poetry and translations were previously collected in two chapbooks, *Tunic*, (speCt! books 2013) a small collection of some of his translations of *Catullus*, and *Coil* (University of Alaska, 1998), winner of the Midnight Sun Chapbook Contest. He lives with his family in Pleasanton, California.

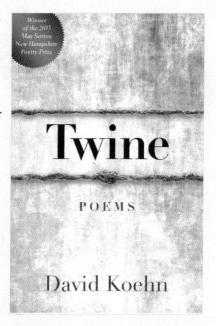

David Koehn's first book, *Twine*, never falters—one strong poem after another. This is the work of a mature poet. His use of detail is not only precise and evocative; it's transformative."
—JEFF FRIEDMAN, 2013 May Sarton New Hampshire Poetry Prize judge and author of *Pretenders*

David Koehn's imagination, rambunctious and abundant, keeps its footing: a sense of balance like his description of fishing: "Feeling the weight . . . of the measurement of air." That sense of weight and air, rhythm and fact, the ethereal and the brutal, animates images like boxers of the bare-fist era: "Hippo-bellied/And bitter, bulbous in their bestiary masks." An original and distinctively musical poet.
—ROBERT PINSKY,
United States Poet Laureate, 1997-2000
and author of *Selected Poems*, among numerous other collections

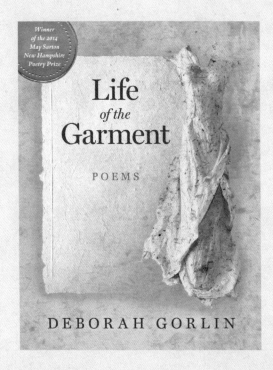

Deborah Gorlin won the 2014 May Sarton New Hampshire Poetry Prize. She has published in *Poetry, Antioch Review, American Poetry Review, Seneca Review, The Massachusetts Review, The Harvard Review, Green Mountains Review, Bomb, Connecticut Review, Women's Review of Books, New England Review,* and *Best Spiritual Writing 2000.* Gorlin also won the 1996 White Pine Poetry Press Prize for her first book of poems, *Bodily Course.* She holds an MFA from the University of California/Irvine. Since 1991, she has taught writing at Hampshire College, where she serves as co-director of the Writing Program. She is currently a poetry editor at *The Massachusetts Review.*

In poem after poem in *Life of the Garment,* Deborah Gorlin clothes us in her fabric of sung words, with characters unique and familiar, and facsimiles of love that open and close their eyes, comfort, and gaze upon us. Read this fine collection—you will see for yourself.
—Gary Margolis, 2014 May Sarton New Hampshire Poetry Prize judge and author of *Raking the Winter Leaves.*

Desirée Alvarez won the 2015 May Sarton New Hampshire Poetry Prize. She is a poet and painter who has received numerous awards for her written and visual work, including the Glenna Luschei Award from *Prairie Schooner*, the Robert D. Richardson Non-Fiction Award from *Denver Quarterly*, and the Willard L. Metcalf Award from the American Academy of Arts and Letters. She has published in *Poetry*, *Boston Review,* and *The Iowa Review*, and received fellowships from Yaddo, Poets House, and New York Foundation for the Arts. Alvarez received her MFA from School of Visual Arts and BA from Wesleyan University. Testing the boundaries of image and language through interdisciplinary work, as a visual poet she exhibits widely and teaches at CUNY, The Juilliard School, and Artists Space.

These poems often shot shivers up my spine. Some made me cry. This is a book I'll want to read over and over.
—Mekeel McBride, 2015 May Sarton New Hampshire Poetry Prize judge and author of *Dog Star Delicatessen: New and Selected Poems*

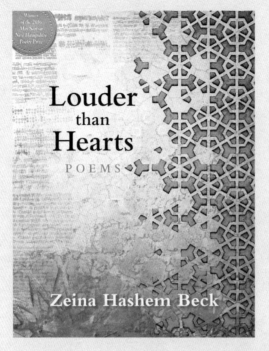

Zeina Hashem Beck won the 2016 May Sarton New Hampshire Poetry Prize. *Louder than Hearts* melds English and Arabic, focusing on language throughout.

Beck is a Lebanese poet. Her first collection, *To Live in Autumn*, won the 2013 Backwaters Prize; her chapbook, *3arabi Song* (2016), won the 2016 Rattle Chapbook Prize, and her chapbook, *There Was and How Much There Was* (2016), was a smith|doorstop Laureate's Choice, selected by Carol Ann Duffy. Her work has won Best of the Net, been nominated for the Pushcart Prize, the Forward Prize, and appeared in *Ploughshares*, *Poetry*, and *The Rialto*, among others. She lives in Dubai and performs her poetry both in the Middle East and internationally.

"I don't know how Zeina Hashem Beck is able to do this. Her poems feel like whole worlds. Potent conversations with the self, the soul, the many landscapes of being, and the news that confounds us all—her poems weave two languages into a perfect fabric of presence, with an almost mystical sense of pacing and power."
                                                                    –Naomi Shihab Nye